For
My three cats:
Maddie, Harriette, and Edward.

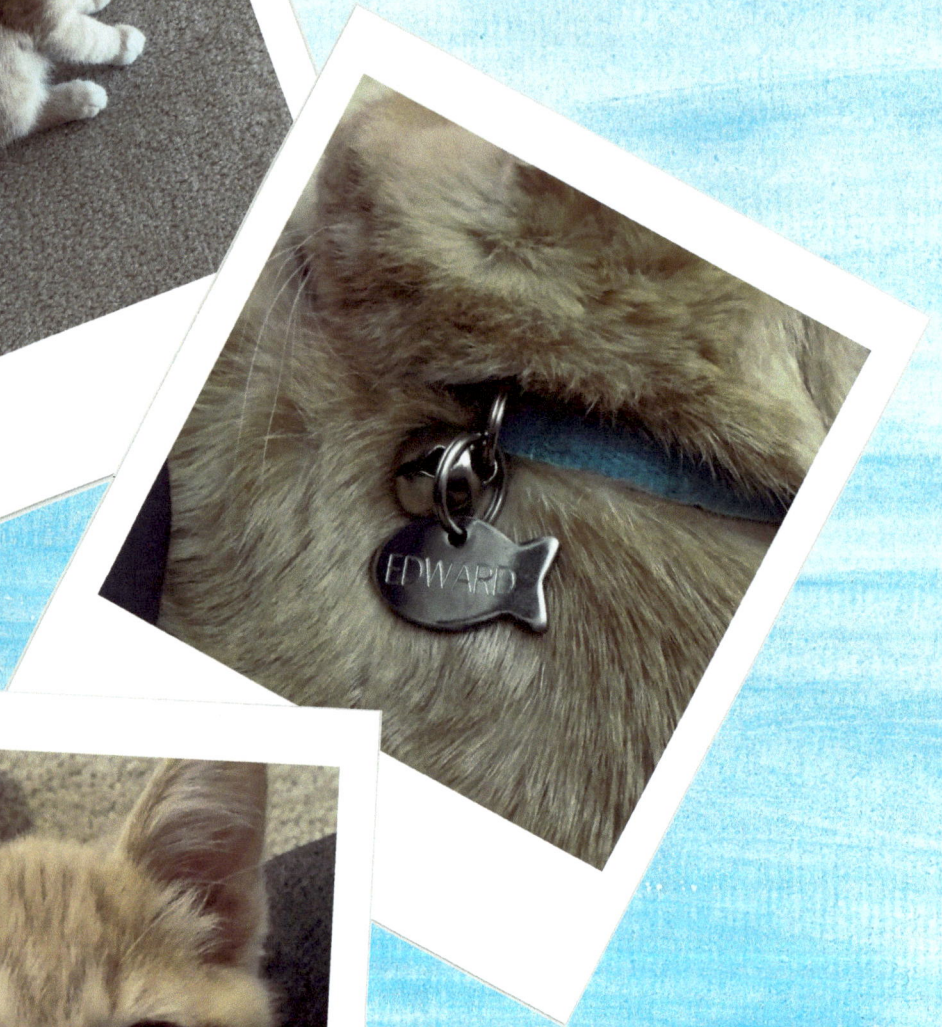
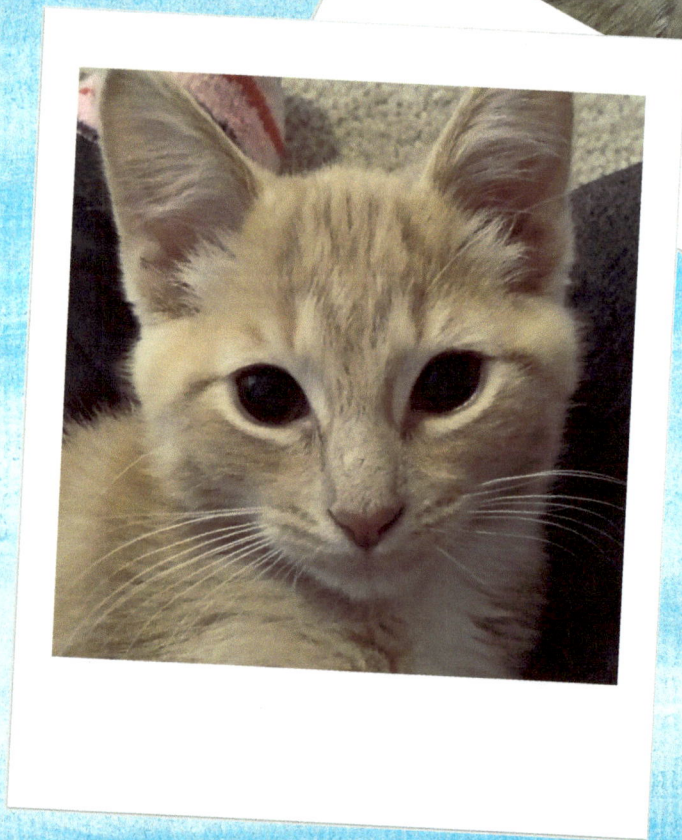

This is Edward.

Here is Edward's story.

There was once a small orange kitten sitting in a cage at an animal shelter.

An animal shelter is a place where animals can go when they have nowhere to live.

He did not have a home yet, or a family of his own.

The orange kitten was not sure how long he would
have to stay at the shelter.

As it turns out, his wait was not long. On the kitten's second day at the shelter a lady came in to look at him.

He stood at the front of his cage, and made sure to look extra cute.

The lady took the kitten out of his cage.

"I came here just for you" she said.

"Your name is going to be Edward, and I'm going to be your new mommy. Time to go home little fella, but first, we have to go see the doctor to make sure you are healthy" said the lady.

After Edward was settled in the car, they drove to see the veterinarian. A veterinarian is a doctor who takes care of animals.

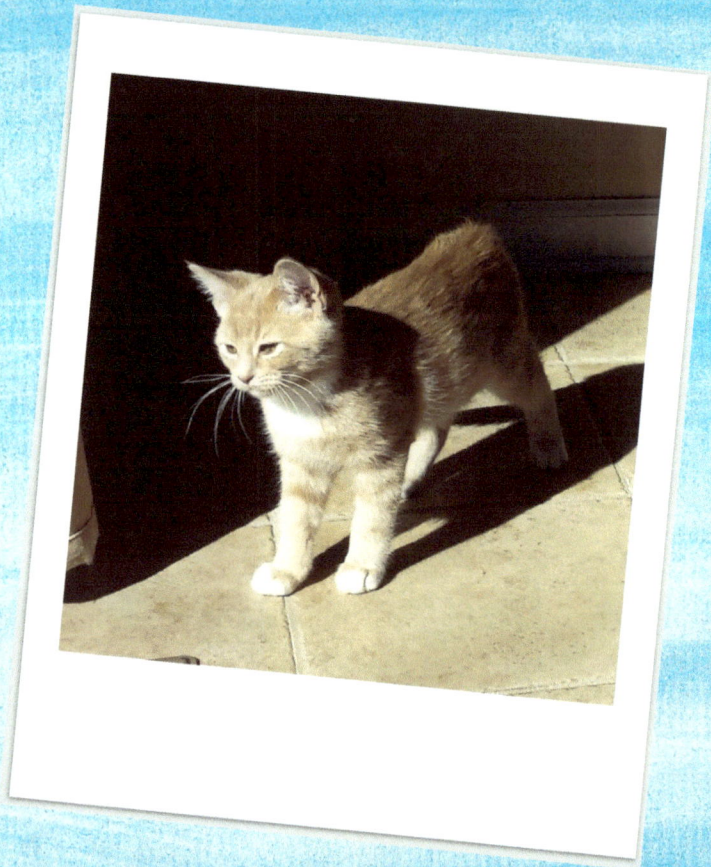

When they arrived, Edward's new mommy took him inside to meet the veterinarian. His name was Dr. G.

After Edward's checkup, Dr. G said Edward was healthy and he could go home.

Mommy put Edward in his carrier, and they got back in the car to go home.

After a while, they pulled into the driveway of a pretty house.

Mommy parked the car in the garage and took Edward inside to see his new home.

Once they were inside, mommy let Edward out of his carrier. His new home was much bigger than his cage at the animal shelter. There were so many new things for him to see.

Mommy took Edward upstairs. At the top, there was a bedroom. Mommy told Edward that this was the cat's room. Inside, mommy showed Edward his food and water bowls, and the way to his litter box.

Edward walked around the room. There were lots of small toys to play with, and bigger toys to climb on. There was even a pile of cozy blankets to sleep on.

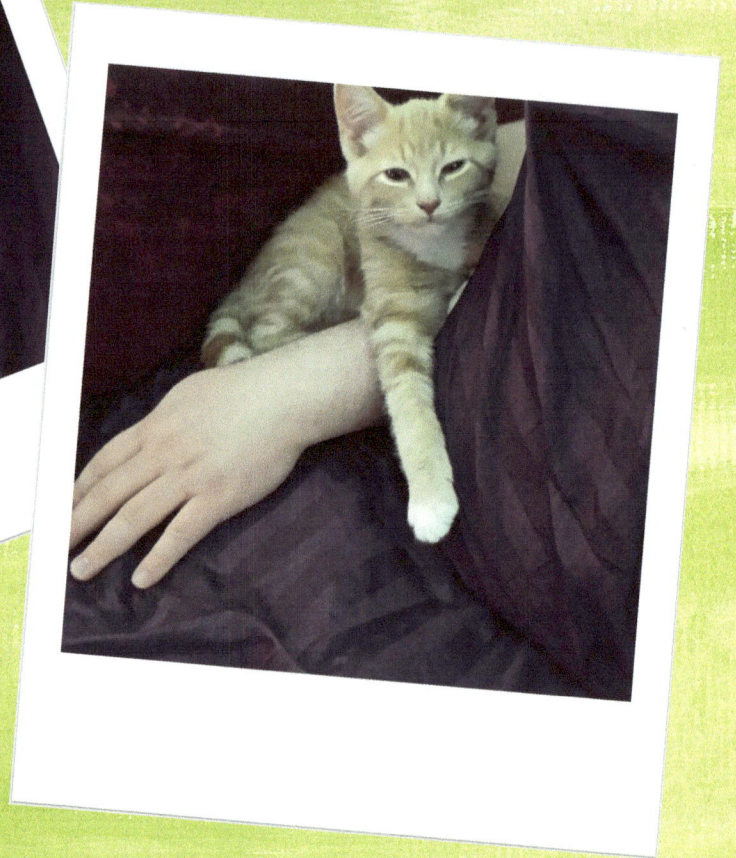

Next, Edward found out that not only did he have a new mommy, but he had a new daddy too. He was nice, just like mommy.

There were two other cats that shared the home as well. Their names were Maddie, and Harriette. Edward liked his new sisters and they liked him too.

Edward found his mommy sitting on the floor. He climbed onto her lap, and laid down. Edward felt very tired. It had been a big day, with lots of things to see and learn. As mommy started to pet Edward, he began to purr. Then he heard his mommy say "Go to sleep little fella, everything is okay. We are your family now, and this is your forever home. We will love you, and take care of you, always, and forever, no matter what."

Edward felt very happy.

Edward now has a mommy, a daddy, two sisters and a home. All together they make a family. Edward is a lucky little fella. Edward sure hopes that all of his friends at the animal shelter find good homes too.

www.ingramcontent.com/pod-product-compliance
Lightning Source LLC
Chambersburg PA
CBHW041237040426
42445CB00004B/64